TO:

_____

FROM:

_____

© 2014 Christian Art Gifts, RSA
Christian Art Gifts Inc., IL, USA

Designed by Christian Art Gifts

Images used under license from Shutterstock.com

ISBN 978-1-4321-1250-9

Printed in China

15 16 17 18 19 20 21 22 23 24 – 12 11 10 9 8 7 6 5 4

Joy

christian
art gifts ®

This is the day
the L ORD has made;
we will rejoice and
be glad in it.

Psalm 118:24

Joy is the experience
of knowing that you are
unconditionally loved.

Henri Nouwen

The joy of the LORD
is your strength.

Nehemiah 8:10

Everyone knows
how to smile. It's one
of the greatest gifts
God has given us.

Joyce Meyer

In Him our hearts
rejoice, for we trust
in His holy name.

Psalm 33:21

There is not one
blade of grass,
there is no color in
this world that is
not intended to
make us rejoice.

John Calvin

Rejoice in the
Lord always.

Philippians 4:4

Keep the joy of loving God in your heart and share this joy with all you meet.

Mother Teresa

When Your words
came, I ate them;
they were my joy and
my heart's delight.

Jeremiah 15:16

May your joys be
as deep as the ocean,
your sorrows as light
as its foam.

Anonymous

The LORD is my
strength and my
shield. My heart leaps
for joy and with my
song I praise Him.

Psalm 28:7

Those who bring sunshine into the lives of others cannot keep it from themselves.

James M. Barrie

May the God
of hope fill you with
all joy and peace as
you trust in Him.

Romans 15:13

Joy is the holy fire
that keeps our purpose
warm and our
intelligence aglow.

Helen Keller

You will go out
in joy and be led
forth in peace.

Isaiah 55:12

The sun does not
shine for a few trees
and flowers, but for the
wide world's joy.

Henry Ward Beecher

My lips will
greatly rejoice
when I sing to You,
and my soul, which
You have redeemed.

Psalm 71:23

Hope fills the afflicted soul with such joy and consolation that it can laugh while tears are in the eye, sigh and sing all in a breath.

William Gurnall

He will yet fill your mouth with laughter and your lips with shouts of joy.

Job 8:21

Joy runs deeper
than despair.

Corrie ten Boom

You turned my
wailing into dancing;
You removed my
sackcloth and clothed
me with joy.

Psalm 30:11

Happy is the person who not only sings, but feels God's eye is on the sparrow, and knows He watches over me.

Alfred A. Montapert

Because You are
my help, I sing in the
shadow of Your wings.

Psalm 63:7

Joy is a net of love by
which you can catch
souls. A joyful heart is
the inevitable result of a
heart burning with love.

Mother Teresa

"Rejoice because
your names are
written in heaven."

Luke 10:20

The purest joy
in the world is joy
in Christ Jesus.

Robert Murray M'Cheyne

Those who look to Him for help will be radiant with joy; no shadow of shame will darken their faces.

Psalm 34:5

Joy is not necessarily
the absence
of suffering, it is the
presence of God.

Sam Storms

With joy you will
draw water from the
wells of salvation.

Isaiah 12:3

True joy comes only from God and He shares this joy with those who walk in fellowship with Him.

Jerry Bridges

You love Him even though you have never seen Him. Though you do not see Him now, you trust Him; and you rejoice with a glorious, inexpressible joy.

1 Peter 1:8

God is most glorified
in us when our
knowledge and
experience of Him
ignite a forest fire of joy
that consumes all
competing pleasures.

Sam Storms

You have given
me greater joy than
those who have
abundant harvests of
grain and new wine.

Psalm 4:7

We rejoice in spite
of our grief,
not in place of it.

Woodrow Kroll

I am overwhelmed with joy in the LORD my God! For He has dressed me with the clothing of salvation and draped me in a robe of righteousness.

Isaiah 61:10

When we are
powerless to do
a thing, it is a great
joy that we can
come and step inside
the ability of Jesus.

Corrie ten Boom

Rejoice always,
pray continually,
give thanks in all
circumstances; for
this is God's will for
you in Christ Jesus.

1 Thessalonians 5:16-18

Joy does not simply happen to us. We have to choose joy and keep choosing it every day.

Henri Nouwen

The precepts of the
LORD are right, giving
joy to the heart.
The commands of the
LORD are radiant,
giving light to the eyes.

Psalm 19:8

Joy is strength.

Mother Teresa

May the righteous
be glad and rejoice
before God; may they
be happy and joyful.

Psalm 68:3

To see God is the promised goal of all our actions and the promised height of all our joys.

St. Augustine

Delight yourself
in the LORD, and He
will give you the
desires of your heart.

Psalm 37:4

Joy is the simplest
form of gratitude.

Karl Barth

Rejoice in the
LORD your God!
For the rain He
sends demonstrates
His faithfulness.

Joel 2:23

It is not how much
we have, but how
much we enjoy, that
makes happiness.

Charles H. Spurgeon

The prospect of the righteous is joy.

Proverbs 10:28

One joy scatters
a hundred grieves.

Proverb

Honor and majesty surround Him; strength and joy fill His dwelling.

1 Chronicles 16:27

It is His joy that
remains in us that
makes our joy full.

A. B. Simpson

Ask and you will receive, and your joy will be complete.

John 16:24

Get hope and get joy,
get joy and get strength.

Rex Rouis

The LORD your God
will bless you in all
your harvest and in
all the work of your
hands, and your joy
will be complete.

Deuteronomy 16:15

You will find a
joy in overcoming
obstacles.

Helen Keller

For His anger lasts
only a moment,
but His favor lasts a
lifetime; weeping may
stay for the night,
but rejoicing comes
in the morning.

Psalm 30:5

Be good, keep your feet dry, your eyes open, your heart at peace and your soul in the joy of Christ.

Thomas Merton

Joyful is the person
who finds wisdom,
the one who gains
understanding.

Proverbs 3:13

Mirth is God's medicine.

Henry Ward Beecher

The Lᴏʀᴅ has
done great things
for us, and we are
filled with joy.

Psalm 126:3

Joy is the serious
business of heaven.

C. S. Lewis

The Holy Spirit produces this kind of fruit in our lives: love, joy, peace, patience, kindness, goodness, faithfulness, gentleness, and self-control.

Galatians 5:22-23

Gratitude changes
the pangs of memory
into a tranquil joy.

Dietrich Bonhoeffer

The kingdom of
God is not a matter
of eating and drinking,
but of righteousness,
peace and joy in the
Holy Spirit.

Romans 14:17

Your success and happiness lies in you. Resolve to keep happy, and your joy and you shall form an invincible host against difficulties.

Helen Keller

His glorious power
will make you patient
and strong enough to
endure anything, and
you will be truly happy.

Colossians 1:11

Prayer should be
the means by which I,
at all times, receive all
that I need, and, for
this reason, be …
my source of rich and
inexhaustible joy in life.

Ole Hallesby

Those who
sow in tears shall
reap in joy.

Psalm 126:5

The reflections on
a day well spent furnish
us with joys more
pleasing than ten
thousand triumphs.

Thomas à Kempis

LORD, You will show
me the path of life;
in Your presence
is fullness of joy;
at Your right hand
are pleasures
forevermore.

Psalm 16:11

Think of all the
beauty still left around
you and be happy.

Anne Frank

Let all those who seek You rejoice and be glad in You; and let those who love Your salvation say continually, "Let God be magnified!"

Psalm 70:4

Joy is the infallible sign of the presence of God.

Pierre Teilhard de Chardin

Light shines on
the godly, and
joy on those whose
hearts are right.

Psalm 97:11

When our lives are filled with peace, faith and joy, people will want to know what we have.

David Jeremiah

God gives wisdom,
knowledge,
and joy to those
who please Him.

Ecclesiastes 2:26

Find joy in
the ordinary.

Max Lucado

Because of our faith,
Christ has brought
us into this place of
undeserved privilege
where we now stand,
and we confidently
and joyfully look
forward to sharing
God's glory.

Romans 5:2

Holy joy will be oil
to the wheels of
our obedience.

Matthew Henry

Glory in His holy name; let the hearts of those who seek the LORD rejoice.

Psalm 105:3

Joy has its springs
deep down inside.
And that spring never
runs dry, no matter what
happens. Only Jesus
gives that joy.

S. D. Gordon

Lord, Your laws are my treasure; they are my heart's delight.

Psalm 119:111

There is no joy in
the world like the
joy of bringing one
soul to Christ.

William Barclay

God is with you,
the Mighty
Warrior who saves.
He will take great
delight in you.

Zephaniah 3:17

To get joy,
we must give it.
To keep joy,
we must scatter it.

John Templeton

The godly will rejoice in the LORD and find shelter in Him. And those who do what is right will praise Him.

Psalm 64:10

The Lord gives His
people perpetual joy
when they walk in
obedience to Him.

Dwight L. Moody

"I will see you again;
then you will rejoice,
and no one can rob
you of that joy."

John 16:22

God intends the
Christian life to be
a life of joy ... those
who walk in holiness
experience true joy.

Jerry Bridges

Shouts of joy and victory resound in the tents of the righteous: "The LORD's right hand has done mighty things!"

Psalm 118:15

No one can get joy by merely asking for it. It is one of the ripest fruits of the Christian life, and, like all fruits, must be grown.

Henry Drummond

Light shines on the righteous and joy on the upright in heart. Rejoice in the LORD, you who are righteous, and praise His holy name.

Psalm 97:11-12

The surest mark of a
Christian is not faith,
or even love, but joy.

Samuel M. Shoemaker

Lord, You will
fill me with joy in
Your presence.

Acts 2:28